THE NEWS: POEMS

 wn

THE NEWS
POEMS

COPPER CANYON PRESS

Port Townsend, Washington

Cover art: Stewart Hardy, *Cathode Ray Tube Watching*
(2014), digital image www.tiltedimage.com

Copper Canyon Press is in residence at Fort Worden State
Park in Port Townsend, Washington, under the auspices of
Centrum. Centrum is a gathering place for artists and cre-
ative thinkers from around the world, students of all ages
and backgrounds, and audiences seeking extraordinary cul-
tural enrichment.

LIBRARY OF CONGRESS CATALOGING-IN-PUBLICATION DATA

Brown, Jeffrey, 1956–
[Poems. Selections]
The news / Jeffrey Brown.
    pages cm
ISBN 978-1-55659-480-9 (pbk.: alk. paper)
1. Journalism—Poetry. I. Title.
PS3602.R6985A6 2015
811´.6—dc23

                                        2014031781

9 8 7 6 5 4 3 2

COPPER CANYON PRESS
Post Office Box 271
Port Townsend, Washington 98368

www.coppercanyonpress.org

For Paula

Contents

PART THREE: THE NEWS FROM HOME

PART FOUR: THE NEWS AT MIDNIGHT

Foreword

Jeffrey Brown in this book apprehends some specific realities: the *news* as a medium and the news that is the medium's object. Brown's poetry examines that material in a new way, giving it a fresh, urgent form. I mean *form* as the term applies to sports or dance: an effective, useful organizing of energy. *The News* is more than a venture into art by someone prominent in another field. In these poems, an unconventional subject for poetry is dealt with from within, by a real poet.

"To see beyond the camera," says Brown about his purpose. The phrase works in two directions. Looking outward, these poems strive to see beyond the camera's instrumental vision of what is before it, the stuff of the daily news: disasters and elections, celebrations and wars, famous artists and notorious criminals. Looking inward, Brown offers a vision from the other side of the camera: the feelings, understandings, and bewilderments of the makers who work behind the instrument, directing and controlling its gaze.

Jeffrey Brown respects his profession. His belief in the value of news reporting, along with his ways of questioning the processes, gives a spine of purpose to *The News*. Jaded skepticism would be trivial, and preening would be even worse. Pride in the work, along with candid fatigue and misgivings, animates the poet's quest to get what the news medium and its devices can see externally and what it can know internally.

Ultimately, this subject matter is as mysterious as culture itself. More immediately, it has immeasurable importance in the political realm, the world of power. Brown treats that world, its eminences and accomplishments, its thugs and abominations, with the passionate, lyrical understatement of a onetime classics major.

For example, in the first, dedicatory poem, within the span of eleven lines there is a credible, human-scale exchange of words between two people—traveler and hotel porter—along with a sense of the planet itself, in its astronomical scale. That concentrated vision of the local and the global is achieved partly by how the poem's final words, "a wider world. // And you in it, you carried in it," echo an earlier stanza:

> Uniformed, night-shifted
> a man crossing borders
> in the satellite's beam—

The satellite's beam, transmitting news of the world, possibly illuminating as well, prepares the scale of the "wider world" one can enter, and be helplessly carried by: the human, social world and the planet, both irresistibly, necessarily in motion, reflected by rhythms of stanza and line.

Another example of art, from "Haiti":

> La Saline—the giant slum
> on a sun-soaked shit-soaked morning
> as the children filled their buckets
> from a makeshift well. The pigs
> scavenged while a rat watched
> all. Why bother to hide?

The approximately three-beat lines begin with a rational juncture after "giant slum" and the same, a little more rapid, after "shit-soaked morning," then more rapid again as the sentence strides across the line break, noun to verb, on "The pigs / scavenged," and ending at the most violent enjambment: "while a rat watched / all." The tension between line and sentence, reflecting the tension between poetry and fact, increases steadily. In the space between the observer and these plague-menaced children, the emotion builds.

More than once, the poems deal with extreme situations by

letting someone in the place and *of* the place have the last word. "Haiti" ends not with the poet's voice but with the words of a man whose son was among the many who died: "I am a bird left without / a branch to land on." Another poem, "Taha Muhammad Ali," cites the Arab poet, who has said, "No 'Palestine,' no 'Israel' in my poetry /... but 'suffering, longing, pain, fear.'" Taha Muhammad Ali, in the poem's last words, presents a question: "Do you know the meaning of a meal?" This artful resolution by quoting, or attribution, is partly the resource of an expert interviewer. It is also a way of resisting resolution, a gesture away from various frames—the newsman's viewfinder or screen, the poet's page or stanza—toward the actual, bewildered, or bewildering texture of one person's experience.

That focus on particular lives also governs the sequence "Honor Roll," which attends to particular soldiers and marines. Their deaths are against the backgrounds of Afghanistan and Iraq, along with the reported and imagined texture of each individual. The poems of the sequence are as direct and plain as snapshots.

The News also includes poems based on the poet's own life. Others are based on professional conversations with artists, including Mark Morris and Philip Roth. At the center of all, implicitly or explicitly, is the main concern: trying to see past the surface, past what the camera can show or mean. The recurring action is one of deferral rather than arrival—an acknowledgment that the very act of observing, every necessary effort to report, creates its own distortions. The last poem in the book, again set in Haiti, again ends with the words of someone other than the poet:

> In Kacite they passed out purification tablets
> displayed with pride their new latrine.
>
> A woman sweeping her dusty steps—
> asked to act naturally for the camera

to act as though we're not here—
more honest and aware than us, replied:
How can I pretend that you are not here?
Was that not you who spoke just now?

By honoring the human voice, Jeffrey Brown has brought a remarkable, fresh kind of attention to these questions of identity and presence, delusion and awareness—in the specific realm of television news and in life itself.

Robert Pinsky

THE NEWS: POEMS

Dedication

To the porter in a Tucson hotel
who took my bag and asked:
Do you yourself love poetry?

Uniformed, night-shifted
a man crossing borders
in the satellite's beam—

and now, he said, a reader of poems.

Chance and change in a desert hotel.
Imagine him there, the porter
imagining a wider world.

And you in it, you carried in it.

PART ONE: NIGHTLY NEWS

Nightly News

Consider the camera, its gaze
as long as the cloudless night
focused yet false, distorted.

Hear the story of the air
the voices straining to breathe
the sound of sand sifting away.

Ask yourself the questions:
Who what when where
and why is the sky suddenly ash?

Why the laughter, why the dead
what the child said when asked
who and where and why?

Clarity, cliché—polished package
that wraps the unwrappable.
Here it is, your day.

Song: Lead Story

If it bleeds it leads
and if it bleeds it feeds
the want of eyes
and I who bring you
this festival of fear

If it bleeds it leads
and if it bleeds it sees
the devouring eyes
and I who recite you
this carnival of crime

If it bleeds it leads
and if it bleeds it reads
the hunger of eyes
and I who offer you
this parade of pain

If it bleeds it leads
and if it bleeds it needs
the sanction of eyes
and I who perform you
this theater of theft

If it bleeds it leads
and if it bleeds it heeds
the fickleness of eyes
and I who play you
this symphony of sin

If it bled it led
the broken the dead
the aversion of eyes
and I who sing you
this lyric of loss

Haiti

"Epidemiologically this area is terrifying"
La Saline—the giant slum
on a sun-soaked shit-soaked morning
as the children filled their buckets
from a makeshift well. The pigs
scavenged while a rat watched
all. Why bother to hide?

La Saline: somewhere nearby
the assaulted salted sea.

Days later, the last light high
in the Central Plateau so far so
bone-crushed by the road (I'd
argued against going), Saut d'Eau.
They filled the benches
and told us of death upon death.
A man who'd lost his son:
"I am a bird left without
a branch to land on."

Beirut

"This is the family tradition: my father
killed by his bodyguards, his father

killed. They chose sides, chose right
and then wrong and he who longs for

the security of death in his bed must
leave this country. My son knows this

and his will too." Within the same frame
the eye deceives, meanings hide when

you stand outside this history. What
I'd thought was construction, a building

with views toward the sea, on the rise,
was its opposite, destruction: pockmarked,

see-through, gun-wrecked Holiday Inn,
monument against forgetting. Restaurants

filled, kebabs on the grill, and on this day
jets in Gaza, far to the south. In the south

of this city, craters from other jets
left, again, unfilled, while a billboard

touts the Party of God. Permission
required to aim the camera, granted by

Hezbollah—watching us watching them
watching them watching us, and all know

who controls these streets. Later I walk the
Corniche, in this Paris of the Middle East—

was it ever so? Two decades of war—
from *Little Mountain:* "We were looking

for the sea." Look again, so close, here!
And there, can it be? The familiar choice

of chocolate or glazed, no wrong or right.
Hezbollah by day, Dunkin' Donuts at night.

Auden saw it in Brueghel's Icarus:
within the same frame, tragedy plus

a girl eating ice cream, strawberry.
This is what we encounter, too: memories

that encompass craters and bombed hotels,
faces red with hate at the jets overhead.

But also the sound of the oud, the light
in the park, nervous fathers watching for falls.

Joplin

A staircase
in an open field
leading nowhere

÷

Scenes that make no
sense—landmarks gone
street signs lifted and flung
into the next county

÷

Trees
a gasp of breath
so grim so beautiful

÷

Your own block
looks like no block
your own house
no longer a house

÷

"The first thing
I picked up
in my parents' yard

was a pendulum
then: Monopoly hotels
a bullet
the clock"

÷

Trees like knives
aimed at a placid sky

Headlines 1

Bomb Explodes in a Crowded Market
Winds blow, my friends are scattered

Dow Falls on Jobs Numbers
I add and add and it doesn't add up

President to Address the Nation
I seek a way out, a way in—away

White Smoke: Habemus Papam
I turned for a moment—where did she go?

U.S. Demands End to Cyber Attacks
I've forgotten every book I've read

Detroit: Crisis Born of Bad Decisions
This is the life I choose now

News Flow

The principle is simple:
one thing leads to another
direct flow of facts A to Z
this source that place those notes
checked and confirmed, imperative
of the next and it begins again.

The gadgets reassure
all is right with the world
when the satellite sends
words from here to forever
the underground lines
transmit nothing but the truth.

But what of the missed cue
a look away a blank thought
garbage in garbage out
the poor choice the daydream
that unravels the day and
leads to nowhere nights?

Wrong place at the wrong time
this truth and not that one
the hand that shakes under
the desk the slimmest veneer
of understanding by those
who give and those who receive.

Let it go: it goes its own way
passing this on passing that off.

West Point

Backpacks on benches
caps on their hooks

all stand to attention
for the professor of poetry

who mapped today's lesson plan:
death and honor at Thermopylae

the Somme, Hamburger Hill
and the names we now announce:

Baghdad, Fallujah, Najaf
Kabul, Khost, Korengal.

Will reciting a sonnet
make me a better lieutenant?

This is what they ask
of Shelley, of Owen

the clearest words, a step away
from "a bleeding world"

measuring war by meter
command by rhyme, killing

by form, victory by the time
it takes to read one's way

from Troy to Kandahar where
today the bomb explodes.

"We're here," the cadet says,
"to learn to take lives"

and art serves, we all serve
an arc of humanity in death

the ancient brutality of battle
muck and muse, books and blood.

"The most powerful tool
a soldier has," the general writes

"is not his weapon but his mind"
and art—cadets on the march—

calls forth what is best
even as men do their worst.

Rain Shadow Review

Locked down, confined, the latest lines
by the poets of the Arizona prison system

high-security Rincon Unit outside Tucson
orange jumpsuits and number 2 pencils

a writing workshop, the week's reward in a place
"not conducive to the truth," it can hurt you bad.

Armed robbery, manslaughter, assault, murder
reciting their works, past and present

rough men, bleak room, kind words, one
hour's refuge in a "human garbage dump."

Roll call of wrongs, under the influence
of drugs, drink, ideology, gangs

stupidity, fear, and whatever, wrong
and wrong again. Still, the teacher said

"If you can learn to use the language honestly
you can apply it to yourself honestly."

He speaks, listens, gathers up the books—
the desert descending outside.

Impossible to ignore when the *Review* arrives
that I was there for a day, five years before

and there they remain.

Campaign 2012

1. Wisconsin

Somewhere in this state
there are twenty-three voters
yet to make up their minds.
The rest chose long ago.
Political signs for this one or that
yard to yard and on the overpass
above I-94 outside Milwaukee
the horns honk, thumbs
and middle fingers raised, the
sun, the wind, the noise
the trucks so close we could
reach out and touch them
jump aboard, take to the road
escape it all, escape it all.

In Oconomowoc (learn to say it)
the superintendent of schools
wants to "use our resources better"
and one of those, a teacher
asks how his kind have become
"public enemy number one."
Peter Yarrow sings for the troops—
he is still singing. A collective
bargaining, Tea Party
the *Progressive*, loud and bitter
choose your side, in this proud
laboratory of democracy.
A boot of beer at Mader's

a search party sent out
for the twenty-three souls
who cannot or will not decide.

2. North Carolina

In central Durham
the old tobacco plant
an upscale Historic District
of fine food and shops.
In Rocky Mount
the textile mill
shuttered, a broken
American landscape.
(The issues here?
"Jobs, jobs, jobs—that
would be your top three.")
In the Raleigh rain
women awaiting a shampoo
but "fired up and ready to go."

The retail game of American
politics: door knocks, phone calls
on the streets and in the pews
living room coffees, small
and then large rallies, to
drive the vote, win the race
a joyous and painful sport.

Along the way I took my hits
for the team in the ring
at the Cageside gym—a mixed
martial artist (why "artist"?)

who feared his friends might
not turn out this time:
"When I kick," he said—thwack!
"I'm kicking through the person."

European Union

"Europe Dodges a Crisis in Spain
but Perils Lurk" across the continent.

A pitiful game of who's-the-jerk
who gambled and lost my retirement?

An addiction to borrowed money
a contagion of bubbles burst

inevitable laws of boom and bust
yet no one imagined the worst.

Fiscal integration—a dream and a lie
in Madrid and Athens it's sung.

Take *that* to the bank, Mr. Minister
in any continental tongue.

Intervention

From high on the hill we searched the valley
for water, right to left, until—there!
A small lake, man-made by the look of it
too perfect, a reservoir perhaps, an
early hike before entering the day.

A front-page photograph that same morning:
solitary man walking through
a destroyed Syrian town, oddly
familiar, the man, as though I'd seen or
known him, his hike from somewhere

to nowhere. Perhaps he, too, was seeking water.
On our descent, the rain came. Boots
on the ground, deep impression in
the muddy earth, a silent prayer: please
accept our well-intentioned footprints.

Song of the News

What do we see
and what do we say?
Between what happened
and who cares?
Between give a damn
and what the hell.
Between good evening
and good day—
car crash
caress
the children at play.
All that we see
and all that we say.

PART TWO: QUESTIONS

The Art of the Interview

1

Engaged, open, curious, firm
prepared by all
that's come before, no
surprises but ready
to be surprised again.

So much we don't know
will never know.
A voice inside
your head ticking
down the seconds.

Ask the question, listen
ask again, expect
an answer, listen, then
ask again, listen for
doubt, resolve, some truth.

As though one could climb
inside another's brain.
So much we don't know
tick—don't ask—tick
don't want to know—tick.

2

Once a man froze
unable to speak.

I asked and answered
every question myself
then said: "You agree?"
We could have gone
on forever.

Another night the lights
went out. We understood
we were still, again
always in the dark.

    3

It was cooler than usual
in August, when the heat
here sticks to your gut.
A question held in the air
ready to burst, then
pop pop pop—and out.

It was cooler than usual
and the night air was
still, still listening
as the moon grew large
raised its white face and
said, *Let me ask you this:*

Philip Roth

"There's a dummy who lives here, too"
pointing to his head
meaning: who knows
where tales come from
and why this worked and how?

I smiled at the time
and even then noted the "too"
that small appendage
of intention and certainty
talent sharpened and hard-earned.

Another dummy—me:
what was it your ambition to do?
(So many dumb questions.)
Tell us a story, true or not
of a page, a sentence, a word.

Later, his hand on his book:
"People won't read these things
in twenty-five years."
When we are done, it too
literature, the lost cause.

Several months later, midair
a flight attendant told me
Roth looked so sad and wise
meaning: do you think he's right?
No, I thought, not while dummies live.

Taha Muhammad Ali

There are two kinds of language, Taha says
one for the poet and one for the news.

So he reads the papers and writes his lines
and the world rests while he drinks his tea.

What a face—that nose! As though he'd come
to blows with every pilgrim in Nazareth.

In his shop I see my grandfather
trading family stories with a neighbor

while that sharp eye hawks the customer—
the "G"—staring at the jewelry.

Buyer wonders: Will she love? Should I pay?
Seller asks: What is the price of contentment?

Taha is a rich man from a razed world
the earth thick with blood and trinkets.

Now he lives with Steinbeck and Shakespeare
one half-expects them to appear for falafel.

No "Palestine," no "Israel" in my poetry
he says, but "suffering, longing, pain, fear"

put it together and there: Israel and Palestine
down through time, down through tears.

(How long does it take, I ask, to grasp
the wonder of water, the blessing of bread?)

But enough, he says—the crooked smile—
my wife expects us, we can't be late.

We wake, we fight, the same every day
then to my shop, four hours of peace

until home for a lunch that is...
perfect, filling, a feast for the gods.

Forty-seven years, unhappily wed!
Do you know the meaning of a meal?

Mark Morris

Put on a dress
had a Coke and a smoke.

"My assignment was to make a dance
that was evocative and mysterious

and seemed like people had been
doing it for ten thousand years."

The music always first
first move in the first note

last step in the last sound.
The dance an expression

of what is said in the melody
the rhythm, the ecstatic

structure of an oratorio
or country-western song.

Ten years later I saw
L'Allegro, the best response to

What is art, what calls it forth?
(A teacher standing before us

said "the answer
to poetry is poetry.")

Pattern within pattern
"though you may not see it."

All in motion and all motion
stopped in place.

"Not cold, just clear."
Not cold, just clear.

And who gave you that assignment?
"Me. I gave me that assignment."

Headlines 2

Justices Weigh Issue of Patents on Human Genes
I wandered lost, until you walked through the door

U.S. Feeds Syrians, but Discreetly
Lies and deceit, lies and deceit

Obama's Agenda at a Crucial Juncture
There are many ways this could end

Bombing Inquiry Turns to Motive
What is it that you want? she asks

Europeans Reach Deal with Google
I'll stay, I'll go

The Day After, Combing for Clues
The day after, combing for clues

Richard Avedon

Look around you: all gone
all dead. The heavy-lidded,
snake-charmed, sunbaked.
The poets and actors, Capote
with the blotched face, Marilyn
in sequins, Beckett and one
of his drifters, the powerful
and the pretenders.

They stood before a white screen
as close to me as you are now—
a confrontation that will last.
Eyes closed tight and eyes alert.
Eyes ahead and eyes askew,
as though they knew not to stare
at the viewer—click!—forever.
All gone, all dead—forever.

This is why I call the taking
of portraits a sad art, he said.
The camera lies all the time,
it's all it does is lie. But this
is no lie: over there, my father—
Sarasota, August 25, 1973,
staring at me, forever. He does
not age. But he will not return.

Gore Vidal

"Always a godfather, never a god"

That was Vidal, at least
as told to me by his friend
the day that he died
amid honors and barbs.

A great line, though who knows
when the flim starts flamming
who said what, really
and when and to whom?

I once played straight man (hah!)
to the great man.
He knew me not and
deigned to know no more.

Told me with a sigh
of the grand old times:
guest on the *Today* show
and that night, with "John."

Sad what we come to
never beating the odds.
An evening with yours truly
a man, not a god.

Suzanne Farrell: September 10, 2001

Rise and fall, the pursuit
of possibility and failure.

The flight the leap the arc
the expectation of air

where all existence hangs on
"how alive your eyes are."

Was it true we'd forgotten
how to be vulnerable?

To open our minds and watch
as bodies float through space?

And then it came, steel and dust
dream and drama, a holding

of breath as terrible
and beautiful as she'd said.

And you, I asked her:
If I could wave a magic wand

and make your body whole
would you dare to dance again?

And she, smiling for the first
and only time, answered:

"Where's your wand?"

Brice Marden

Colored dirt on a surface
that's all it is
doing the same damn thing
for forty thousand years.

Pulverized powder
mix and stir
the material nature of paint
cave, canvas, image, absence.

A complicated visual
experience, an ancient
command: Look
hard at something.

Neanderthal

"a possibility that Neanderthals were the artists"

JOHN NOBLE WILFORD, *NEW YORK TIMES*

1

Red disk, handprint
patterns from nature
symbols of power and prayer.

You know this story:
history is written
by the winners.

But wait now: who
is this *we*? The
portrait's all wrong.

The huge forehead
a no-brainer
or so we thought

some primal pride
in our own lineage.
Who else can do

what we do, walk
and chew gum
at the same time?

First rough draft
check our facts
fog of war

mix our metaphors
and our media
could it be—art?

    2

This is how I see him
lurching from the cave:
Pablo Neanderthal

animal skins a riot
of splattered paint
the happiest mess

of any almost-man
who ever walked
the great earth.

Museum of Modern Art

"Unthinkable at one moment... practically compulsory in the next"

PETER SCHJELDAHL, *THE NEW YORKER*

Unthinkable at one moment
compulsory the next
history not long after.

Maker of marks, making one's mark
on time, while the rest of us
stumble through it.

÷

I am an abstraction, the abstract painter said.
And you are my distraction, the man inside my head.

÷

In the distance beyond the vivid mountains
the blue becomes blue becomes another blue.

Unthinkable at one moment...
practically compulsory in the next.

But here, now, in this moment:

No invention no strategy no compulsion.
We are free to wander in that free blue space.

There at the horizon is where
the painting begins.

Night

Raven at the window
is this my true face?

River birches swaying
is this my true name?

Who sings the song
that flows through the night?

"A faraway place
and a place close at hand"—

Why is the hour
never enough?

Interview

To whom am I speaking?
Why do you ask?
I ask the questions!
Ask what can be answered
Why set limits?
Is that your question?
Have we spoken before?
I believe we have

I watched a river birch
Was it bending toward the sun?
Movement and its absence
Did a woman walk past?
Summer's hissing and whistling
Did she stop and smile?
The bark, the leaves, a breeze
Let me ask you this:

When did you first know?
I'm still not sure I do
And when was it all clear?
I'm still not sure it is
Does the birch feel the sun?
Warmth and its absence
And if I turn and turn?
Then you turn, you turn

At night sometimes I stare
Are there stars? Is there light?
"Your hair upon the pillow"
Can you find your own words?
A looking and a looking back
What are you looking for?
Yes there is light and yes it is dark
Have you ever told the truth?

What's the use of asking?
What's the use of asking?
I ask the questions!
Try to get them right
And if I know the answers?
Can that be the point?
We've spoken before? We will again?
I believe we have, I'm certain we will

PART THREE: **THE NEWS FROM HOME**

Letters to the Editor

The kind, perceptive woman
an angel, who wrote on a Monday:

"Mr. Brown is so emotionally present"
Why did you find it so funny?

The reprehensible pedant
a scold, who wrote on a Tuesday:

"Learn your ass from your Elgin"
You said it: He's lost his marbles.

The well-intentioned economist
an expert, who wrote on a Wednesday:

"Schumpeter would have saved us"
You hissed at his Hayek, razed his Keynes.

The know-it-all grammarian
a stickler, who wrote on a Thursday:

"We expect so much better..."
You split yours, I dangled mine.

The self-righteous cleric
a believer, who wrote on a Friday:

"He must read my treatise!"
Oh, so enlightened! What's under his robes?

And the one with good reason—
you, with a weekend complaint.

A mild upbraiding
then: "Go watch your game."

Voice

for Robert MacNeil and Jim Lehrer

There are those with a voice so rich,
so bell-strong, time-chiseled, and alive
they can read the phone book and
you will hear the deeds and failings
in every name, the laughter and wailing
of ghosts who inhabit each address,
the infinite possibility

in every number. There are those
with a voice *that* rich, he says—
the lucky ones. But that is not us.
We open our mouths and out comes a
small, high sound, cracking midsentence,
straining to tell the story we know
to be true. There are things you can do:

Learn to breathe. Stand up straight and
let the air flow through you, belly to
chest and into the mask of your face.
Take a bite of chocolate, sip on your
coffee—excite the senses. Imagine
the people in their homes hungry for
dinner and for news of the world.

Underline phrases, emphasize what
should be emphasized, diminish the
less important. Decide what is

important. Be sure you understand
the meaning of what you are to say.
Do not yell, do not whisper, look ahead,
not down, fill your lungs, open your mouth

and speak. The Zen master says "You
find your voice when you find yourself."
But that, too, is not for us. (Who knows
what else you'll find *there*? he laughs).
Better to listen to that voice
as though from afar, as though it
is not yours. Then speak again.

The Influence of Anxiety

In the Uffizi, after a *del giorno* meal, we saw
Morandi doing Rembrandt and—keep walking—
Rembrandt doing Morandi, if that is possible.
P and I walking in circles, etchings that seemed
somehow inevitable, no matter where we started.
Momentary anxiety followed by a kind of ecstasy.

It came back, what had set me on fire
so long ago. No surprise now, those courtiers
in hats and sly smiles, soldiers in battle with flags
flying, the Fra Angelico beauty who might step
off the wall into the piazza—keep dreaming—
I was nineteen and language seemed no barrier.

Battles and beauty? Norman O. Brown
took a word, *polemos*, beyond "war" to "strife"
"struggle" through time: Apollo chasing Daphne
into centuries to come (he'll never catch her).
One thing—keep running—leading to another
in myth, literature, and, by the way, journalism.

We—reporters, *anchors*—borrow daily
switching between the breathlessness
of the "new" and "nothing new under the sun."
You think no one's seen or said this before?
Listen! This is important—keep talking—
the green light is on and so are you.

I hear it as I drive: on *Mermaid Avenue*
Tweedy does Dylan doing Guthrie. Listen to
"Airline to Heaven," you think: There he is, no
there *he* is and back and forth, raising the question—
keep singing—of how this one learned, that one
borrowed, and great artists out-and-out steal.

How to take then make yours? The problem
hanging over the head of every would-be
word- and song- and image-maker—keep making.
So much more than just the blank page.
Rather, not blank at all but filled and filled
to overflow with what has come before.

But where was I? Riding down the highway
with Bragg listening to Bob listening to
Woody listening to—keep listening—who?
Some nameless local hero perhaps, so many
ur-men of music who deserve the applause
but in history float like ghosts on page zero.

We met in song, P and I, walking in circles
in search of each other: Homer in Greek
my apartment, Book Two, catalogue of ships
translating lines, touching hands—keep touching—
some anxiety, then ecstasy that was, I swear
original, brought together by a blind bard

singing, sung, sung again, by one and all.

Sam Brown

Pop Sam died watching CNBC
his mind in a muddle
the remote, the TV, the non-
talking head of the market watch.

What difference to him
where it closed that day
up or down when he passed
away from the market watch?

Plumped on his pillow with the
Nasdaq and Dow, and memories
of how investments went south
proud bull of the market watch.

Dreams of a killing, his stocks
and his bonds, not yet willing
to pass on his losses and his
gains from the market watch.

A new high, the final bell
a new low, in the black in the red
my grandfather splayed on
a bed before the market watch.

I wonder now if his risk
was rewarded, a final sale
before the tally recorded
facing the night of the market watch.

I asked him then: Do you know
what this means? He nodded and
smiled and looked serene in the
glow of the market watch.

Side Effects

Those Etruscan couples in forever-embrace
a model for all, unless they too
present a brave face in their passage
between worlds, concealing their potion?
(But see how they grin!)

Today: the happy, gray couple, no worries
no concerns, prancing through fields, glowing
from the sun and having, it's clear, just
done it and knowing—yes!—it can be done again.

Four-hour erection? A hard night indeed
of coupling and pleasure and tumbling together.
Then eyes open to a new sleepless day
but whoa, wait, stay! What? It rises once more!

Deep thrusts and fine print, matrimonial bed
with a hint of nostalgia, suggestion of heat.
Caresses, kisses, climaxes, sighs—
dizziness, nausea, back pain, hives.

May cause moans and may cause aches.
May cause tenderness, may cause flu.
May cause rapture, may cause death—
but that, of course, the Etruscans knew.

Television: An Argument

Still a wasteland, you said.
Did you think I'd disagree?
All the truth and integrity
of a plastic whistle, red
loud and obnoxious
in servitude to silliness
a paean to the obvious—
Have another drink
I swear I'm not proud.

Wires in a box, strangling
the brain, a parody of speech
the talking head talking lies
each speaking to his own side.
All hail the gods of punditry!
And—no, don't say it—Snooki!
What *would* Murrow think?
I despair, cover my eyes—
Pass me that drink.

But, wait, hold on here:
Remember how we watched
Hill Street, ahead of its time?
Furillo to the public defender:
"You give good succor."
Was that not a line worthy
of some bard determined
to lift up, even
embolden the small screen?

Fast forward: Bada Bing!
Age of *Sopranos* and *The Wire*
a tale of two Americas—one has
lots of shows, Simon told me, his
is for the other. A Mad Man with
ambition beyond good and evil of old.
Old? We sit, we watch, we rest
from the day. Our favorite
series ends and another begins.

Headlines 3

Watch Was Urged for Bomb Suspect
The night, cool air, surrounded us

Psychiatry's Revamped Guidebook Fuels Debate
I asked why? Who? In what other life it happened?

In Egypt, a War over Identity
That line from a film, long ago

Scientists Trace Memories of Things That Never Happened
You were always there, my love, always

Turning Hurricane Sandy's Scars into Badges of Survival
I am sick so often, too often, the fever comes

The Dark Side, Carefully Masked
The dark side, carefully masked

Memory

Where is the line
he asks
between short- and
long-term memory?

He is losing
one of them
at least
and seeks definition

clear boundaries
markers, scales
to measure holes
vacancy, absence.

"Dementia care
cost is projected
to double
by 2040."

Baby boomers
like babies
who've left few
to watch over them

living longer—
the good news—
but: "It's going to
swamp the system"

very bad news
for the system and
for my father
debating himself

over the line
between short
and long, long-
and short-term

memory.

Succession

One morning state police
escort us to your grave
the next my flight is canceled.

Maintenance issues breaking
out all over. You would speak
of a "grand theory," something

tying all this together, but
you had none yourself, none
that reached me then or now

as I drive your car slowly
into the tranquil streets
of my youth. Here is where

I learned to ride a bike, on
this high hill that is no
hill at all. And still I fell.

And now you descend and
still I fall. And here is where
I learned to doubt, in the chapel

where we donned black skullcaps
that meant nothing, I tell you.
If god speaks it is elsewhere.

And here are my own children
rooted and uncertain
watching me speak to you.

You watched the news every night
worried if I did not make "air"—
traveling, sick, useless, lost.

Now that you are gone—
traffic parted by the state police—
can I, too, disappear?

The News inside His Head

If I stopped playing, I'd start thinking, and if I start
thinking, I'll die.

DAVID OISTRAKH AS QUOTED BY GIDON KREMER
IN *THE VIOLIN*, BY DAVID SCHOENBAUM

If I stopped playing, I'd start thinking
and where would that get me?
Just thoughts and not sounds
fears and not notes
just "what if" and "who to be"
and not the impossible clarity of these strings
I've made mine, me, mine.

If I stopped working, I'd start thinking
and where would that get me?
Just time and not deeds
dread and not feats
just "what for lunch" and "count the days"
and not the fiery displays of this instrument
I've made mine, me, mine.

If I stopped loving, I'd start thinking
and where would that get me?
Just doubts and not ease
rough dreams and no rest
just "why alone" and "who to see"
and not the settled certainty of this life
I've made mine, me, mine.

If I start thinking, I'll die, I say
and where would that get me?
A man who can't play
there and not here
just "devil take it" and "this can't be"
and not the tangled melody of all
I've made mine, me, mine.

Channel One: Guide

There is a place on the dial
for us all: food, football

scores and highlights
of madness and mayhem

history, heartache, and home—
which way is home?

Order, possibility, a call of the roll
that scrolls down and down forever.

A beginning, new beginning
continuous beginning.

Manual, scripture, an escort
for the lost, lending purpose.

Suppose you fought for ten years
and took ten more to return—

What guide? What direction
when every direction calls?

Old movies and new music
religion and revelation

sci-fi, sitcoms, westerns
horror, vampires so sensitive

so sexy, reality edited for reality
and how much reality can one take?

A place to buy and sell
to leer, smell, and behold

the pundits of democracy
its malcontents, its magnificence.

The embrace of scale and magnitude—
999 and it goes on and on and on.

I who was lost, let me be found.
The remote, a dream of control

on Channel One, my guide.

Cortona

As when a man stands at the window
and squints his eyes to see:
Is it raining?
What fills the space
from here to the horizon?

He sees the drops
descending, the wet
and willful world
so clear before him.

Later, eyes closing tighter
the sky itself disappears.
The light of his life
is no more.

Forecast

Tomorrow I begin my life.
Today, pain and sorrow
but tomorrow
I will open my eyes
wake with no burden
begin again
as the great globe spins.

There will be sun
and there will be clouds.
I will lift my head
touch the one who sleeps near.
Foolishness and greed of men
sanctified somehow
in the familiar bed
in the morning air.

Colors of spring
and colors of fall
we will gather them all
and then—fail again.

The ways of death
love, suffering, joy.
Pain and sorrow
sorrow and wonder
alive in this world
as tomorrow we
begin again.

PART FOUR: **THE NEWS AT MIDNIGHT**

Theater of War

The sergeant said:
To see someone
without an arm or leg
you know what is wrong.
But what if what's missing
is inside. Who sees?

Think back and then
look out at these faces:
the wounded and might-as-well-be
the steady and straight hold-on-to-me
with traces of the hero
before and after

etched in the skin
in a theater of war
and the lack of—what?
Not courage, not heart
not family or memory—
the demon, itself.

Another: Over and over
I wonder what made him
feel so hopeless.

My name is a sad song.
Who would have thought
it would one day become
the sound

a man makes
in despair?

Sophocles was a general
in the Athenian army
so who knows where
the war ends
and the art begins?
(And who will write
our wars?)

The actor tells me:
They lean forward.
They listen
and cry.
And the room changes
like the penny has dropped.

Ajax killed men
and then animals
thinking they were men.
Then he killed himself
thinking he was
less than a man.

Honor Roll

The shed he built in the backyard
the small hole in the right rear corner
that needed repair
his first Harley helmet on a hook.
The plan: Bring in each child—four now—
as they come of age
strap on the gear and scream like a banshee.
Initiation into their father's world.

The grenade in Kunar ended that.
It was December, with Christmas coming.

Like a train roaring through the trees
the loudest sound you ever heard
then doubled and doubled again
and you wonder: Where is the sound?
What is the sound? How can this be?

A known prankster
this whole thing a bit of a lark.
Loved to tickle his young wife's toes
in the dark, until she woke, annoyed
and then warm and then so warm
and then kissing and another sort of play.

Tried a trick on his platoon sergeant
with other results expected.
Expectations met—still, a good joke.

Death found him laughing in Fallujah.
Bullets shattered his shoulder, then spine
then all. A smile on his lips, then quiet.

Like a child blowing bubbles
delighted by air
until one pops and she learns
for the first time: Everything
may not turn out all right.

3. ARMY PRIVATE ND: IRAQ, 2007

Had the softest touch, the ball
drop drop dropping through the hoop.
The pride of her tribe, a warrior
on the court and then in a foreign land

where her war whoop delighted
her new band of sisters and brothers.
Played there, too, and won money
in H-O-R-S-E: a hook, a jumper, swish!

Until in Diyala one shot missed
and another rang true.
Now the game back home
is played in a dark arena of sorrow.

Barely here and so much here—
then gone.
Like a butterfly without effort
all grace and light.

Drove his mother crazy
unable to sit still.
What now?
Where this time?
Diving into the quarry
from the highest rock
racing the car at night
on the edge of town
blasting the radio
louder and louder
and lashing out
at every slight.

Where is he now, O gods?
Demon-driven, mother-feared
now smeared over some Afghan road.

Like the storm that never stops
darkening day into night
drowning cities and men.

5. ARMY PRIVATE JG: IRAQ, 2006

His last ride, the airport
into town, shotgun in the
armor-plated vehicle
hunk of junk, strap in, hold on.

Could barely hear himself think
or scream—go ahead, scream—
and this he loved on the roller coaster
back home, arms flapping, hair raised.

Saw movement in the shadow
just before the explosion hit.
Amusement park, my ass, he said
tasting metal in a foreign ditch.

Like a dog that rushes into the waves
eyes shining, fur flying
until the sea rises up
and takes him away.

History

At a clearer time
from a greater distance
when the confusion has faded
the battle long done
the lies cut down like
wheat in late summer
in this very field
of human harvests—

then you will know
what happened here
you, so frightened now
and you, so fearsome.

Obituary

I used to laugh and say
the death of this or that
great one was "good news"—
meaning, good for the news.

To sing, to write, to act
to think, to make, to do—
to limn a life, to spin
a tale of time and deeds

a good obituary
imitating a good life
with its beginning
middle and end

unlike life itself
or how we perceive it
one accident piled
on the last—and then past.

I should have been
a writer of obits
town crier of death
chronicler of fates

filling in details
wondering at gaps
counting the survivors
closing the books.

When I go, no need
to write it down, just
say: I was yours.
Oh—and music please.

And if you go first (please don't)
then I shall shudder
and shake, hope and wait
for a calm hand to write:

This was the news
about me and you—
a beginning, a middle
and now, my love, an end.

Poetry and Prose

After much
reflection
I have decided
to respectfully
decline
your offer.
I am grateful
you were willing
to put your
confidence in me.
And there was
a big part
of me ready
and eager
to take on
the challenge.
But I am
unable
to meet your
requirements.

Haiti: Kacite

We, who lie, who cannot say—
for there is no good way to put this—
we are here to show the horror of your life.

In Kacite they passed out purification tablets
displayed with pride their new latrine.

A woman sweeping her dusty steps—
asked to act naturally for the camera
to act as though we're not here—
more honest and aware than us, replied:
How can I pretend that you are not here?
Was that not you who spoke just now?

Afterword

The daily news is a greedy monster that must be fed. I learned that long ago when I stumbled, accident upon accident, into the occupation of journalism. I had no plan. Indeed, everything that resembled a plan led in other directions. But I liked to write, liked to learn, liked to look, sometimes even liked to talk to people. All that narrowed things down a bit and then the gods had their fun. And still do.

But the news? The *daily* news? *Television* news! Of the reporter's classic questions—who, what, when, where, why—only one is easily answered. Who? Me. The rest remain open, swirling, occasionally breaking through to stir up the night. There's no time to dwell on the questions, on the answers, on anything really. It's another day. What do we do now? Time to feed the monster.

The news tells us what happened. *We* tell *you* what happened. The story of the day: The bomb exploded, the stock market imploded, the bad guys conspired, the good ones expired. Journalism comes with a history, rules, its own language (at times giving way to cliché), a prescribed form of presentation.

Television journalism has its own traditional forms: an "anchor" (hold fast) sits at a desk in a studio (today, often pacing about) and calmly (today, often breathlessly) announces the important events of the day. It is constructed to be authoritative, assuring. But it is also a performance. Like the actor onstage, the anchor reaches through the camera to say: Listen to me! Let me tell you a story.

We are "reporters." Town criers in the public square, witnesses to secret affairs. We look, observe, take notes. We ask questions, check facts, write, speak, tell it. To report: we *bring* it. (And like the porter in a Tucson hotel, we carry baggage.)

We tell a true story. We try to get it right. We try very hard to get it right. Our credibility is on the line. Will you credit us? Trust us?

Watch us? Not if you don't believe us. So hear me now, tonight, on the news: This is a true story—as true as we can make it in this moment.

Yes, the moment. The practice of daily journalism is bound by time: twenty-four hours, one hour, one minute, last second. When I sit in a television studio, there is a voice in my head—the director's—counting down the time: "Four, two, one, gotta go!" Do you know how long a minute actually is? I mean, how *short* and *long* one minute can be? If it happened yesterday, we don't care today. If it happened this morning, how does it feel tonight? The news is "up to the minute," 24/7, one cycle followed by the next. Start, finish, begin again. Live, on the air, in real time.

Voices, within and without. In that television studio, *inside the news*: your own internal monologue as you interview someone: What did he just say? What do I ask next? When am I supposed to pick up my kids? How much time is left? External voices: They come from across the table, from the mouth of the person you are speaking to. They come through the camera, that person seen but not seeing. And they come from the mouths and minds of a million viewers—taking it in, on the couch, eating dinner, listening intently or hardly at all, talking to a spouse, talking *back* to the television, talking to themselves (a million internal monologues added to your own). Voices endless, continuous.

We leave the studio. We go "into the field," out in the world, where events are unfolding, people living, fighting, building, doing. We go where news is being made. The enormous privilege of this: we are able to go places most people cannot go, to enter into the lives of others to a degree that runs the range from enlightening and transformative to painful and embarrassing; we're able to ask questions that genuinely interest us of people who have compelling, even important things to say.

And so, as in these pages:

> Haiti, a year after the earthquake: The rubble was still everywhere, though in neater piles. The despair in the tent camps

was growing, the realization had hit that this was no temporary solution. And now, cholera. It had started in the rural central highlands and swept down into the cities.

Beirut: On the flight over I read Elias Khoury's *Little Mountain*, a short novel set amid the brutal fighting, street by street, during Lebanon's fifteen-year civil war. And then I was walking those same streets, alive with life, but signs everywhere of the ferocity of battles, bombings, and assassinations layered through time.

The Theater of War: An auditorium on a military base. Ancient Greek tragedy adapted and presented to American soldiers and marines. The U.S. military today faces an epidemic of PTSD and suicide. More than two thousand years ago Sophocles spoke to it.

A dancer, a painter, a woman who lost her home in a tornado, a child in a classroom, government officials and taxi drivers. And the dead—of horrible disease, mass shootings, the common and "unknown" causes listed in the obituary section I so love to read in the daily paper. The fallen soldiers we remember in our honor roll at the end of our program: "Here, in silence, are five more."

All of it and so much more, here and not here, day after day, the events, the voices, the images, captured on camera, reported as it happened, told to you—the news.

÷

Then, why poetry? The news is contained in and by its form. Done well, it has a beginning, middle, and end. It is complete. It *feels* complete in its moment. And yet even as we turn off the television or close the newspaper or shut down the tablet we know—should know, must know—that we have experienced just one sliver of the story, of the "what happened."

The photographer Richard Avedon once said to me, "The camera lies all the time. It's all it does is lie." He was putting it dramatically to make his meaning clear: the photographer chooses this moment, not that one, this image, not that one. Here, in the viewfinder, is one thing. Widen out, shift left or right, perhaps something quite different. The camera captures one truth, but just one of many potential truths.

It is of course the same for our cameras and our words on the nightly news. Bound by time, by strictures of form, language, and more, how else could it be? This scene and not that one, this sound bite and not that one, this way of describing and not that one. We strive for objectivity—a goal I believe in—even as we understand the subjective source and nature of the telling. The truth of the moment is always at least slightly askew, if only because—as the woman in a small village in Haiti's highlands pointed out, we are there. And "I" the reporter—I am a husband, father, son, employee, American, and many other things. If I am a witness to what happened, what I see and say is shaped from a mix of identities, memories, meanings.

No time to stop, I said earlier. But do stop, just a moment, and it becomes so clear: we experience the world in multiple ways, at multiple levels. In the field, at a desk, through books, in the eyes of the one we love, in our dreams—just to name a few—and we can express that experience in multiple ways.

Poetry is one way, a way I came to as a reader long ago. *The Iliad* was and is for me a living record, thrillingly told, of how we humans fight, suffer, love, make heroes and fools of ourselves. Lyric poetry through the ages has offered the purest expression of the interior lives of men and women and what happens between them. Journalism *uses* the language. And good journalism—including television news—uses it very well, indeed. But poetry *frees* the language.

The poem seeks and creates its own form. Meaning matters, yes. But so do sounds, shapes, and rhythms. And they open our eyes and minds to what is in front of us and, sometimes, what is behind and beyond that.

Poetry through time and across time zones: I've sought it out on the page and wherever I've gone as an expression of place and people. I've also sought out poets—amazingly (even to me), it's a part of my job.

And so, here:

Taha Muhammad Ali, in his trinket shop in Nazareth, spoke of the two languages, one for the news and one for the poet. And it was clear—from spending time with him, from reading his work—that his life was an act of reconciliation of those languages as well as of peoples in a troubled land.

Two poetry classes: one in a high-security prison in Arizona, the other for cadets at West Point. They have almost nothing in common except dedicated teachers and participants in highly regimented institutions who *choose* to spend time with literature, and, most of all, the highest imaginable stakes.

Poets have sought—and I like the very human, striving quality of this—to understand just what it is they're doing, just what their place is in the world. Octavio Paz writes:

Between what I see and what I say,
between what I say and what I keep silent,
between what I keep silent and what I dream,
between what I dream and what I forget:
poetry.

Seamus Heaney speaks of poetry's power and responsibility to "redress." And in a line of prose that suggests what we might aspire to, he writes: "I wanted to affirm that within our individual selves we can reconcile two orders of knowledge which we might call the practical and the poetic; to affirm also that each form of knowledge redresses the other and that the frontier between them is there for the crossing."

See it, report it, say it. Now cross the frontier and do it again, shake and stir, seek other words and rhythms. The news anew.

÷

The program I work for occupies an important but small niche in the media universe. It's a good place to be. We have a decent-sized, passionate following of people interested in what's going on around the planet. We don't live in the realm of mass-market celebrity— I walk through large swaths of the world anonymously—but people I don't know walk up to me on the street all the time and say, "I have dinner with you every night." ("What are we having tonight?" I ask.) Some recall one story or another, one interview or another, and say, "You have the best job in the world." (The response depends on the day. On good ones, it's, "Shhh, don't tell anyone.") Some say or write a version of: "How could you be such an idiot, a hack, a fool, a lackey!" (The answer to this does NOT depend on the day.)

I've also had people come up to say that the work I do has made a difference in their lives. The poem "Dedication" reflects one such moment, a chance encounter, when a hotel worker told me he'd never read poetry until he watched me talking to poets and having them read their work on television. "You got me into it," he said. "You got me hooked." This is gratifying beyond all words.

I got hooked as a reader a long time ago. But why write poetry? Why write these experiences through poetry? To explore what happened from another angle, to see beyond the camera, to imagine what might be there, to use the language in a different way. Like the news, poetry seeks to inform our lives and helps us to reflect upon who we are and the conditions, disastrous or delightful, of the world in which we live. Here it is—I am talking to myself, again—your day.

Acknowledgments

The News is a work of the imagination that is grounded in the very real world of the news. The former is all mine. The latter I have shared for more than two decades with many wonderful colleagues and friends at *PBS NewsHour*. My love and gratitude to you all, and special thanks to those who were part of the experiences captured in this book: Mary Jo Brooks, Anne Davenport, Murrey Jacobson, Joanne Elgart Jennings, Mike Melia, and Terry Rubin.

I'm grateful to all who allowed me into their lives—the subjects and makers of news. In addition to those mentioned by name in the poems and those who, for various reasons, cannot be named, I thank Bryan Doerries, the actors and the military personnel who took part in Theater of War at Fort Myer in Arlington, Virginia; Richard Shelton and the inmates in his workshop at the Rincon Unit of the Arizona State Prison Complex in Tucson; and Elizabeth Samet and the cadets in her West Point class.

Thank you to Michael Wiegers and everyone at Copper Canyon for taking this on and for the care you've given it. I've long admired the work you do and couldn't be more pleased to be a small part of it.

This book would not have been possible without the encouragement and guidance of Robert Pinsky—great friend and teacher. Thank you, Robert, for a master class in your "singing school."

To my mother, Miriam, and in memory of my father, Morton, who died during the writing of this book.

To my children, Sophie and Jack, who are somehow no longer children. Have I told you? You're there in every line.

Above and beyond, to Paula Crawford, partner in all things and always.

About the Author

Jeffrey Brown is a senior correspondent for *PBS NewsHour*. In a twenty-five year career with the program, he has anchored the nightly newscast, served as arts correspondent, and reported on a wide variety of stories from around the world. *The News* is his first book.

Poetry is vital to language and living. Since 1972, Copper Canyon Press has published extraordinary poetry from around the world to engage the imaginations and intellects of readers, writers, booksellers, librarians, teachers, students, and donors.

WE ARE GRATEFUL FOR THE MAJOR SUPPORT PROVIDED BY:

THE PAUL G. ALLEN FAMILY FOUNDATION

 CULTURE   Lannan

 THE MAURER FAMILY FOUNDATION
OFFICE OF ARTS & CULTURE
SEATTLE

 WASHINGTON STATE ARTS COMMISSION

Anonymous

John Branch

Diana Broze

Beroz Ferrell & The Point, llc

Janet and Les Cox

Mimi Gardner Gates

Linda Gerrard and Walter Parsons

Gull Industries, Inc.
   on behalf of William and
   Ruth True

Mark Hamilton and Suzie Rapp

Carolyn and Robert Hedin

Steven Myron Holl

Lakeside Industries, Inc.
   on behalf of Jeanne Marie Lee

Maureen Lee and Mark Busto

Brice Marden

Ellie Mathews and Carl Youngmann
   as The North Press

H. Stewart Parker

Penny and Jerry Peabody

John Phillips and Anne O'Donnell

Joseph C. Roberts

Cynthia Lovelace Sears and
   Frank Buxton

The Seattle Foundation

Kim and Jeff Seely

Dan Waggoner

C.D. Wright and Forrest Gander

Charles and Barbara Wright

The dedicated interns and faithful volunteers of Copper Canyon Press

TO LEARN MORE ABOUT UNDERWRITING COPPER CANYON PRESS TITLES,
PLEASE CALL 360 385-4925 EXT. 103

The Chinese character for poetry is made up of two parts: "word" and "temple." It also serves as pressmark for Copper Canyon Press.

✢

The interior is set in Miller, a "Scotch Roman" designed by Matthew Carter in 1997. The display type is set in Gotham, designed by Tobias Frere-Jones (2000), inspired by American vernacular signage. Book design by VJB/Scribe. Printed on archival-quality paper.